Shields &
Shards &
Stitches &
Songs

Shields &
Shards &
Stitches &
Songs

Dan
Beachy-
Quick

OMNIDAWN PUBLISHING
RICHMOND, CALIFORNIA
2015

Cover design: Alex Jovanovich

Interior design: Gillian Olivia Blythe Hamel

Typefaces: OneSlot and Joanna Std

Offset printed in the United States
by Edwards Brothers Malloy, Ann Arbor, Michigan
On 55# Heritage Book Cream
Acid Free Archival Quality Recycled Paper
with Rainbow FSC Certified Colored End Papers

Published by Omnidawn Publishing, Richmond, California
www.omnidawn.com   (510) 237-5472   (800) 792-4957
10 9 8 7 6 5 4 3 2 1
ISBN: 978-1-63243-007-6

Shield

Be of ruin this rude maker.
Rubble be. Ruin be. Be not a stone.
Hellstone. Hailstone. Hellebore
Take root in the broken and bloom.
Bloom blood into bitter lake
Or let dirt drink its fill. The bee moans
In its thin cup. Pollen and trouble.
Mark it in bronze, poet. Grab the tool. Beat it.

Shield

Omen. Ailment. What
The prayer moment intones.
The god-itch. And the electric fields
When spring plugs yellow in and water sings.
Bring the cup. Bring the potsherd.
Read the broken name. The
Moon is an example of the
Shut door seeking a key. Wild sea. Open.

Shield

You be awe. I'll be knife.
There's an altar by the water.
You be creature. I'll be priest.
Slack sails wait wind. Wind waits feast.
Least blood most blessed. You be what I lack.
Ceased asking why. Ceased open eyes. You
Alter in darkness alone. My girl of gold-hair-
Life. Be antlers of deer. Be your own rescue.

Shield

No goat song. No satyr.
No dancing cloven hoof. No stiff prick.
No wine-drunk Silenus singing love sick.
No cyclops. No shepherds. Nothing but a stick.
Wreck the bronze by beating it. Throw
Brick. Throw spear. Throw
Shit from stables. Let worms gnaw all. Go
Gather harm and bring a little home.

Shard

Be   maker.
    be   be   stone
                         bore
         the broken
       blood
      drink its   moans
    thin   trouble
        poet   tool

Shard

                    wo   wo
                    the   cloud
         bee a   a
      field
shut   down, wh   y
         grant blades
see   shroud . Lash
      to   a   . Use

Shard

        o let

not   o

   eyes.   eyes. See

     the wet   grass

                 wait.

took a cloud for

     me. In mist

  a   refuge.

Shard

       O   What

       pray   o   o

god   .   the elect

                       sing

    the   the

        broken   me. The

Moon is a

hut   or   a   sea.

Shard

                        o mouth
          o eyes   o body
     You   to make   it
                                          dark
                                          shut

           Tight the   lack
     Study   it through.
                your   breath. Re

Shard

awe.

water.

You

wait . Wind
You

ask   why   You
Alter   dark
antlers of   rescue

Shard

song
No   No
No   love
No   Nothing but
        the
        Brick.   Throw
    it   all. Go
                        home.

Stitch

a
tone
o

moan
o
poet

Stitch

                  o

                      loud

   bee

i

     own

    g   lades

                ash

    a   Use

Stitch

o

no   o

yes

we

wait

for

refuge

Stitch

What

god   .

                                          in

the

broke

Moon s

hut   a   sea

Stitch

o

yes

You   make   it

lack

breath

29

Stitch

we

a

wait

You

You

ark

of   rescue

Stitch

on

love

No hing

e

.

all

home

Song

Sing gold this chain's scorched links.
Balm the scathed ear's wounded tone by muting the dove's
Limited cry, *who or who or who or*
Who into becoming so much less through the gray channel
Of her sun-lit sometimes radiant purple-flecked throat.
Beneath cloud a flake of green also moans. Makes moan.
Other heroes also pull their prisons in chains behind.
Heroes other than doves. A kind of poet. A kind of storm cloud. A wound.

Song

The wars are everywhere, o even within.
Drawn in poor bee by the dance loud hum
Of some other tribe, poor bee. Even the center, even the heart,
Keeps a sting sharp: art stings thought, thought stings art.
Petty realm of the long known. Are there other ways to learn to sing?
Clash of long dead blades in the fallow fields
And the wind that blows truce for an hour whistles loud the rash
Martial tune. Some scribe handles himself. "Use it," sings the song.

Song

Image of the Gorgon's eyes into bronze beaten,
Eyes no man can see. Image of Cyclops
Chanting yes as he hammers thunder into a bolt.
Imagine the far west deeps where in ocean dragons roam.
Image of the dragon's teeth in dry ground sown.
Awful beauty of the shields. Cannot say wait
So mime the monster back to fury's face forever
If forever could be real. Solace of eyes
Other eyes hide behind. Lightning's light. Refuge of stone.

Song

Closed circuit of the war chant: what what what.
Words go on forever even after the mouth singing them dies.
Like some god singing in the air. Of clouds. Of horses.
Of wild manes in fog. Of tails tipped in mist.
Before sleep the child speaks: you can't bite rocks
Or you get broke teeth. You can't bite knives.
Moon is too hard. Sun too hot. The sky
Is a hut god built, that's all. Floating above the sea.

Song

Music spills out the unguarded
Mouth, "yes yes" goes the song. The war dent
You suffered, Mind, make some heart beat it out,
Even mine might do, to the very edge,
To make the surface smooth. Like the ocean
When it was new and the wind waited slack in a pale bag
In the first dark before the sun knew it could rise. Then it rises.
Then water gleams. A bright shield breath breaks.

Song

The sun god stood wet in the rain. Modesty, myth.
The missing arm points at the truth or plucks a string
And waits for the tune. The broken penis
Bends down. You know so much
More than you've lived. That's how it feels. You
Prepare remarks, a kind of proof, mostly benign.
Almost no place sees you. Broke the nose off. Dumb form of rescue.

Song

To put the moon back in a song. To put back the sun
And the stars. To loosen a little the air from the ether.
To let the grass keep in thin shadows secret its secret love.
To keep the roots dark. Nothing
Hasn't had enough of fear. Wants fear a little more wild.
To the deaf ear and the wheat ear that cannot not hear the covering pall
Cover up the moon. Find some song like a coin lost in the grass. Give it a home.

Poems in this book previously appeared in the Academy of American Poets "Poem-a-Day" series and in *Fogged Clarity* (which includes an interview about the project). Thank you to Alex Jovanovich for reading these poems, considering them, and creating a work of art in return.

Dan Beachy-Quick is a poet, essayist, and occasional novelist.
He is the author, most recently, of a study on Keats: *A Brighter Word
than Bright: Keats at Work*. He is a Monfort Professor at Colorado State
University where he teaches in the MFA in Creative Writing Program.